100

things you should know about

ARMS &
ARMOR

100
things you should know about
ARMS &
ARMOR

Rupert Matthews

BARNES & NOBLE

NEW YORK

Editorial Director: Belinda Gallagher
Art Director: Jo Brewer
Editor: Rosalind McGuire
Volume Designer: Michelle Cannatella
Indexer: Jane Parker
Reprographics: Anthony Cambray, Stephan Davis,
Liberty Newton, Ian Paulyn
Production Manager: Elizabeth Brunwin

ACKNOWLEDGMENTS
The publishers would like to thank the following
artists who have contributed to this book:
Peter Dennis, Mike Foster, Alan Hancocks, Richard Hook, Angus McBride,
Andrea Morandi, Alex Pang, Carlo Pauletto, Mike Saunders, Mike White
Cover artwork: Mike White

All other artworks are from the Miles Kelly Artwork Bank

The publishers would like to thank the following
sources for the use of their photographs:
Page 43 Ninja Museum, Uemo

All other photographs are from:
Castrol, Corel, digitalSTOCK, digitalvision, John Foxx, PhotoAlto,
PhotoDisc, PhotoEssentials, PhotoPro, Stockbyte

www.mileskelly.net
info@mileskelly.net

ISBN-13: 978-0-7607-9226-1
ISBN-10: 0-7607-9226-7

Printed and bound in China

10 9 8 7 6 5 4 3 2 1

Contents

Weapons of war

1 People have used arms and armor to hunt, defend themselves, and attack other people for thousands of years. Arms are weapons that are carried by a single person. Armor is something that is worn or carried to protect against injury. Early armor was made from wood or leather, and the first arms were made from wood or stone.

▼ At the battle of Lechfeld in AD 955 the Germans crushed the much larger army of Magyars. The Germans succeeded because they were wearing suits of mail armor and carrying new weapons.

The first arms

2 **Some of the first arms were made from stone.** The earliest humans lived hundreds of thousands of years ago. Archeologists (scientists who study the remains of ancient humans) have found weapons made of sharpened stone that were made by these ancient people.

▲ This handax is made from a single piece of stone. It was held in the hand and used with a chopping motion.

3 **Early weapons were used for both hunting and fighting.** Archeologists have found bones from cattle, deer, and mammoths, and discovered that these animals were hunted and killed by ancient people using stone weapons.

► Around 75,000 years ago, spears were made from a stone point, which was attached to a wooden handle with leather straps.

4 **The first warriors did not use armor.** It is thought that early tribes of people fought each other to get control of the best hunting grounds or sources of water. These men may not have used armor, relying instead on dodging out of the way of enemy weapons.

5 **Shields were an early form of defense.**
A thrust from a spear could be stopped by holding
a piece of wood in the way. People soon began to
produce shields made of flat pieces of wood with
a handle on the back. Over the years, shields
came to be produced in many different shapes,
and from a wide range of materials including
metal, wood, and leather.

▲ By about 300 BC, the Celts of Europe
were producing beautiful shields decorated
with bronze and colorful enamel. Some, like
this one found in London, may have been
used in ceremonies.

▶ Flint is a hard stone
that can be chipped and
flaked into a wide variety
of shapes to produce
different types of
weapons, such as these
points or tips for arrows.

6 **Spears were the first effective
weapons.** Many early spears consisted of
a stone point mounted on the end of a
wooden pole. With a spear, a man could
reach his enemy while still out of reach
of the opponent's hand-held weapons. The
earliest known spears are 400,000 years
old and were found in Germany.

I DON'T BELIEVE IT!

The oldest signs of warfare
come from Krapina, Croatia.
Human bones over 120,000
years old have been
found there that
show marks caused
by stone
spearheads.

Ancient civilizations

7 **Early Egyptians may have used their hair as armor.** Some ancient Egyptians grew their hair very long, then plaited it thickly and wrapped it around their heads when going into battle. It is thought that this may have helped protect their heads.

▲ The Egyptian pharaoh Tutankhamun is shown firing a bow while riding in a chariot to attack the enemies of Egypt.

8 **Some Egyptian soldiers had shields that were as big as themselves.** Around 1800 BC, soldiers carried shields that were the height of a man. They hid behind their shields as the enemy attacked, then leapt out to use their spears.

9 Egyptian infantry (foot) soldiers often used axes. Soldiers that served as part of the bodyguard of the pharaoh (king) carried special axes. These weapons were made of bronze and each had a heavy round weight that meant they could deliver a heavier blow in battle.

▲ The curved blade of an Egyptian war ax. The weapon was able to crush any armor or shields in use at the time. This type of ax was used to cut, while other axes were used to pierce armor.

10 Assyrians wore long cloaks of mail. Some soldiers in the Assyrian army wore armor made entirely of mail around 900 BC. This was a series of interlocking metal rings that could withstand blows from swords or spears.

11 Babylonians wore armor that was brightly colored. Around 1000 BC, the ancient city of Babylon, Mesopotamia (now part of modern Iraq), was famous for its wealth. Babylonian soldiers wore armor that they often painted with bright colors to make themselves look more impressive in battle.

▶ An Assyrian army assaults a fortified city in Mesopotamia using siege towers and bows.

Hoplites and phalanxes

12 **Hoplites were armored infantry.** From about 700 BC Greek infantry (foot soldiers) were equipped with a shield, helmet, spear, and sword. They were called "hoplites" ("armoured men"). Each hoplite used his own weapons and armor.

13 **A Greek who lost his shield was a coward.** The shield carried by hoplites was over 3 feet across and made of wood and bronze. It was very heavy, and anyone trying to run away from an enemy would throw it away, so men who lost their shields in battle were often accused of cowardice.

14 **Hoplites fought in formations called phalanxes.** When going into battle, hoplites stood shoulder to shoulder so that their shields overlapped, and pointed their spears forwards over the shields. A phalanx was made up of six or more ranks of hoplites, one behind the other.

▶ The success of Greek soldiers in battle depended on them keeping tightly in formation so that enemy soldiers could not get past the line of shields.

I DON'T BELIEVE IT!

Spartan hoplites were so tough that they reckoned they could easily win any battle, even if they were outnumbered by as many as five to one!

15 Greek spears had a "lizard stabber." Hoplite spears had a bronze spike at the bottom end. This was used to stick the spear upright into the ground and was called a "sauroter," meaning "lizard stabber."

16 The best helmets were made from a single sheet of metal. Skilled metalworkers in the Greek city of Corinth invented a way to make a helmet by beating a sheet of bronze into shape. This produced a helmet that was much stronger than one made of several pieces of metal. The helmets were called "Corinthian."

Roman legions

▲ A Roman legion marches out of a border fortress supervised by the legate, who commands the legion.

17 **Armored infantry formed the legions.** The main fighting formation of the Roman army was the legion, a force of about 6,000 men. Most were equipped with body armor, a helmet, a large rectangular shield, a sword, and a throwing spear.

▶ The armor of a legionary was made up of several pieces, each of which could be replaced if it was damaged.

18 **Roman armor was made of metal strips.** At the height of the Roman Empire, around AD 50 to AD 250, legionaries wore armor called *lorica segmentata*. It was made up of strips of metal that were bent to fit the body, and held together by straps and buckles.

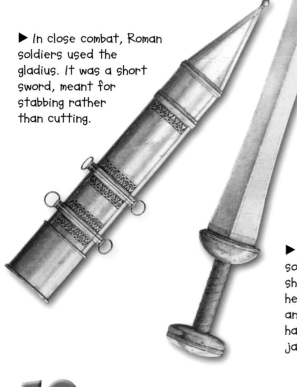

▶ In close combat, Roman soldiers used the gladius. It was a short sword, meant for stabbing rather than cutting.

21 Roman swords were copied from the Spanish.

After 200 BC, Roman soldiers carried swords with straight blades and sharp points. They were copied from swords used by Spanish soldiers who defeated the Romans in battle.

▶ An auxiliary soldier wearing a short mail tunic and helmet, and carrying an oval shield. He has a gladius and javelin as weapons.

19 Roman auxiliaries wore cheaper armor.

Every Roman legion included soldiers called auxiliaries (soldiers from places other than Rome). These units had to provide their own armor, often wearing tunics covered with mail or scale armor, which was made up of lots of small metal plates.

20 Roman shields could form a "tortoise."

One tactic used by the Romans was called the "testudo," or "tortoise." Soldiers formed short lines close together, holding their shields so they interlocked on all sides and overhead, just like the shell of a tortoise. In this formation they could advance on an enemy, safe from spears or arrows.

The fall of Rome

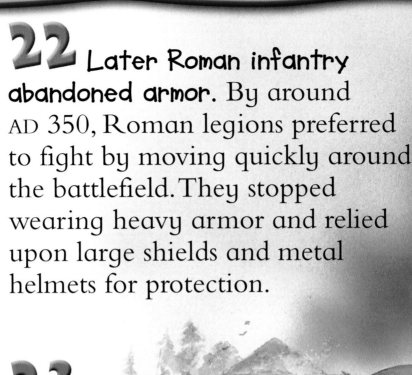

22 **Later Roman infantry abandoned armor.** By around AD 350, Roman legions preferred to fight by moving quickly around the battlefield. They stopped wearing heavy armor and relied upon large shields and metal helmets for protection.

23 **Later Roman armies used mercenary archers.** Roman commanders found that archers were useful for attacking barbarian tribesmen. Few Romans were skilled at archery, so the Romans hired soldiers (mercenaries) from other countries to fight as archers in the Roman army.

24 **Roman shields were brightly coloured.** Each unit in the late Roman army had its own design of shield. Some were decorated with pictures of eagles, scorpions, or dolphins, while others had lightning bolts or spirals.

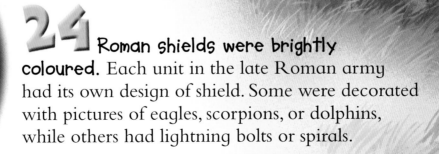

◀ Late Roman shields were brightly decorated. Each unit in the army had its own design.

◀ By about AD 350, Roman armies had large numbers of cavalry that were used to fight fast-moving campaigns.

25 The eagle was a sacred standard.

Each Roman legion had an eagle standard, the *aquila*—a bronze eagle covered in gold leaf mounted on top of a pole about 10 feet long. The *aquila* was thought to be sacred to the gods and it was a great humiliation if it was captured by the enemy.

▶ A Roman *aquilifer* (standard bearer) carrying an eagle standard. Each legion had an eagle standard that was sacred to the gods. Units of cavalry and auxiliaries carried standards of other animals instead of an eagle.

26 Later Roman cavalry had enormous shields.

One later group of Roman mounted soldiers was the *scutati*. These men wore coats of mail, and carried enormous shields with which they were expected to defend themselves and their horses. They would gallop towards the enemy army, throw javelins, and then ride away before the enemy could strike back.

I DON'T BELIEVE IT!

Alaric the Goth and his men looted Rome in 410 AD. Alaric was famously known to carry a sword with a handle made of solid gold.

Gladiators

27 **Gladiators fought in the arena.** Many Roman cities had a building called an arena, which had banks of seating and an oval area in the center covered with sand. The arena was used to stage fights between men known as gladiators, who were trained to fight to the death to please the crowd. They used swords, spears, knives, and other weapons when fighting.

Samnite

28 **Gladiator helmets were large and decorative.** Fights were staged as part of an impressive show. The armor worn by gladiators was decorated with bright feathers, beautiful designs, and may even have been coated with silver or gold leaf.

Thracian

◄ Most gladiator helmets had metal masks to cover and protect the face.

▲ Samnite gladiators used a large shield and short sword, while Thracian gladiators had a small shield and curved sword.

29

Gladiator armor was not designed to save lives. The purpose of these fights was to put on a show of skill with weapons, and the penalty for defeat was death. If a gladiator was wounded in the arms or legs it was unlikely to kill him, but would mean an end to the fight. Some gladiators wore leg and arm armor so that the show could continue for as long as possible.

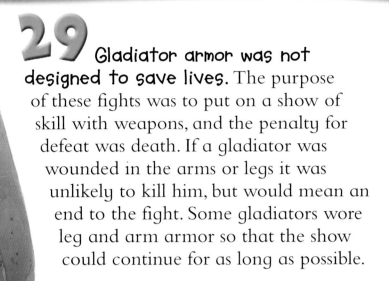

► A helmet worn by an andabata gladiator. It had no eyeholes so the wearer had to fight blind.

▲ The Retiarius was a type of gladiator based on a fisherman, so he carried a net and trident.

30

One type of helmet had no eyeholes. Sometimes gladiator show organizers would make the gladiators wear helmets called andabatae, which covered the eyes, so the gladiators had to rely entirely on their sense of sound.

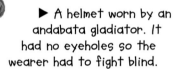

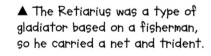

QUIZ

1. Which gladiators fought without being able to see?
2. Which types of gladiator carried a curved sword?
3. What was the name of the building where gladiators fought?

Answers:
1. Andabatae 2. Thracian
3. The arena

19

The Barbarians

31 **Celts used chariots to intimidate the enemy.** Battles between rival Celt tribes often began with famous warriors riding in chariots and performing tricks to show how skilled they were.

32 **The Huns were lightly equipped.** Around the year AD 370 the Huns swept into Europe from Asia. They fought on horseback with bows and spears, but wore no armor. They moved quickly, and showed no mercy.

33 **The Dacian falx was a terrible weapon.** The Dacians lived in what is now Romania around AD 400–600 and fought mostly on foot. Some Dacian warriors carried a long, curved sword with a broad blade that was called a falx. This weapon was so sharp and heavy that it could slice a person in half.

▶ The speed and accuracy of mounted Hun archers terrified the Romans.

34 **The Franks were named after their favorite weapon.** One tribe of Germans who lived around AD 300-600 were famous for using small throwing axes. These weapons had a short haft and a small, square-shaped head and were called "francisca." The men who used them were called franks, and soon the entire tribe took the name. They later gave the name to the country France.

◀ A Dacian warrior carrying a falx. Dacians were a people who lived outside the Roman Empire and often fought the Romans.

QUIZ

1. Did Hun warriors wear armor?
2. What was a "francisca?"
3. Who did the Romans call "barbarians?"

Answers:
1. No 2. A small throwing axe 3. Any uncivilized people who lived outside the Roman Empire

▼ A helmet belonging to an Anglo-Saxon king who ruled in East Anglia, England, about AD 625. It was made of iron and decorated with gold and silver.

35 **Many barbarians wore armor decorated with gold, silver, and precious stones.** "Barbarian" was the Roman name for uncivilized peoples outside the Roman Empire. They loved to show how rich they were and did this to emphasise their status within their tribe.

The Heavenly Kingdom

36 **Chinese troops wore armor made of dozens of metal plates.** The plates were about 3 inches by 2 inches and were sewn onto a leather garment or held together by leather thongs. Around 221 BC the various Chinese states were united. The Chinese believed this unity was the basis of their power and wealth.

37 **Silk shirts helped protect against arrows.** Many Chinese soldiers wore silk shirts under their armor. If an arrow pierced the armor it would drag the silk shirt into the wound without tearing it. By gently pulling on the shirt, the arrow could be extracted cleanly.

▼ A patrol of Chinese soldiers guarding the Great Wall around AD 200.

38 **Crossbows were first used in China.** They were more powerful than the bows used by nomadic tribesmen living north of China, so they were often used by troops manning the northern frontier. Crossbows consist of a short, powerful bow mounted on a wooden shaft and operated by a trigger.

39 **Infantry used pole weapons.** Chinese infantry often carried spears around 6 feet in length. Often an axlike chopping weapon, a slicing blade, or a side spike replaced the spearhead. These weapons allowed the infantry to attack their enemies with a variety of actions to get around shields.

40 **Chinese cavalry were heavily armed.** When patrolling border regions, the Chinese cavalry operated in large formations that could defeat any tribal force causing trouble. The men were equipped with iron helmets and body armor, together with wooden shields and long lances tipped with iron.

QUIZ

1. In what year was China first united?
2. What did Chinese soldiers wear as protection against arrows?
3. Did the nomadic tribesmen live north or south of China?

Answers:
1. 221 BC 2. Silk shirts 3. North of China

The Dark Ages

41 The Dark Ages followed the fall of Rome in AD 410. Barbarian peoples took over the Western Roman Empire, and ancient culture and skills were lost. The Eastern Roman Empire lost power and lands to barbarians, but survived to become the Byzantine Empire. The Byzantines continued to use Roman-style arms and armor.

▲ English warriors patrol the great dyke built by King Offa of Mercia to define the border with Wales in AD 784.

42 English cavalry were lightly armed. Britain was invaded and settled by Germanic tribes from around AD 450, and by around AD 700 they ruled most of the island. Only the richest Englishmen wore body armor. Most went into battle armed with a spear and sword, and carrying a round shield and a helmet as armor.

43 Berserkers wore animal skins instead of armor. Viking warriors were known as "berserkers," meaning "bear-shirts," from their habit of wearing bear or wolf skins in battle.

◀ A Viking berserker attacks dressed in a bear skin. These warriors would fall into a terrible rage in battle and seemed to ignore all danger.

QUIZ

1. Which warriors wore animal skins?
2. Who won the Battle of Lechfeld?
3. Who built a dyke between England and Wales?

Answers:
1. Berserkers
2. The Germans 3. Offa

44 **The battle-ax was a terrible weapon.** Many Scandinavian peoples used a battle-ax that had a haft up to 6 feet long and a blade more than 12 inches across. It was used with both hands. In the hands of a master, it could kill a horse and rider with a single blow.

◀ A Viking raiding party wielding battle-axes attacks a group of Englishmen.

45 **The heavy cavalrymen ruled the battlefield.** In AD 955 a small army of German knights destroyed the larger Magyar cavalry at the Battle of Lechfeld, in Germany. Knights (mounted men in armor carrying a spear and sword) were recognized as the most effective type of soldier.

25

Early knights

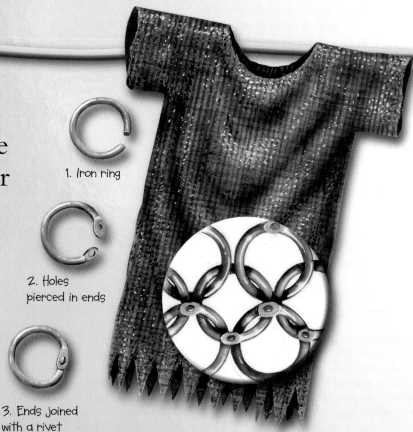

1. Iron ring

2. Holes pierced in ends

3. Ends joined with a rivet

46 **The first knights wore mail armor.** Around the year 1000, most body armor in Europe was made of mail. This was flexible to wear and could stop a sword blow with ease. Such armor was expensive to make so only richer men could afford to wear it.

▲ Mail armor was made by linking together hundreds of small iron rings. The rings could be linked in a number of different ways, just like knitting a sweater.

47 **Shields were decorated to identify their owners.** From about 1150, knights wore helmets that covered their faces for extra protection. Around the same time, they began to paint heraldic designs (coats of arms) on their shields so that they could recognize each other in battle.

48 **Early knights sometimes used leather armor.** Mail armor was effective, but heavy and expensive, so some knights wore armor made of boiled, hardened leather. This was lighter and easier to wear, and was still some defense against attack.

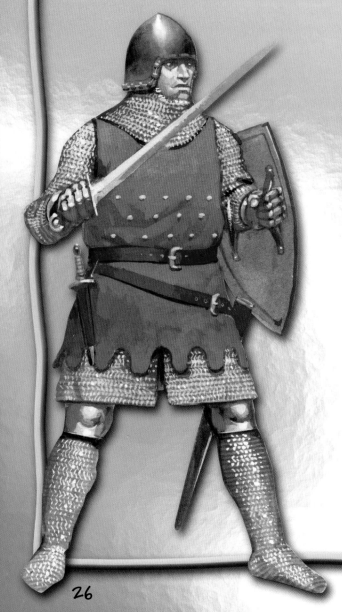

◀ A knight in about 1100. He wears a shirt and trousers made of mail and a helmet shaped from a sheet of steel. His shield is made of wood.

49 **Plate armor gave better protection than mail.** By about 1300, new types of arrow and swords had developed to pierce mail armor. This led to the development of plate armor, made of sheets of steel shaped to fit the body, which arrows and swords could not easily penetrate.

50 **The mace could smash armor to pieces.** The most effective of the crushing weapons developed to destroy plate armor, the mace had a big metal head on a long shaft. A blow from a mace crushed plate armor, breaking the bones of the person wearing it.

The armor around the stomach and groin had to be flexible enough to allow bending and twisting movements

The most complicated section of plate armor was the gauntlet that covered the hands. It might contain 30 pieces of metal

The legs and feet were protected by armor that covered the limbs entirely

▶ A suit of plate armor made in Europe in the early 14th century.

Archers and peasants

51 **Infantry were usually poorly armed.** Around 1000 years ago, ordinary farmers or craftsmen would turn out to protect their homes against an enemy army. Such men could not afford armor and usually carried just a spear and a large knife or an ax. They usually guarded castles and towns.

▼ A Welsh spearman in about 1350. He carries a spear and sword, but has no armor at all.

◄ An English archer in about 1400. He wears a metal helmet and has quilted body armor.

52 **The longbow was a deadly weapon.** From about 1320 the English included thousands of archers in their armies. The archers were trained to shoot up to eight arrows each minute, producing a deadly rain of arrows that could slaughter an enemy force at a distance.

53 **Some weapons were based on farming tools.** Many soldiers used weapons that were simply specialized forms of farming tools. The bill was based on a hedge-trimmer but could be used to pull a knight from his horse, and then smash through his plate armor.

▲ The heads of an English bill (left) and Dutch godendag (right). Both were pole weapons used by infantrymen.

54 **Crossbows were used in some countries.** Soldiers from Italy, the Low Countries, (now Belgium and the Netherlands) and some other areas of Europe preferred to use the crossbow instead of the bow. It could not shoot as quickly, but was easier to learn how to use and much more powerful.

55 **Some foot soldiers wore armor.** Infantrymen sent to war by wealthy towns or cities were often equipped with armor. They usually formed solid formations with their long spears pointing forward, and could be highly effective in battle.

◄ A crossbowman would hide behind a large shield called a pavise while reloading his weapon.

Make a castle bookmark

You will need:
card • scissors • crayons • sticky tape

1. Draw a tower 5 inches tall on card and cut it out.

2. Draw the top half of a soldier holding a shield on card and cut it out.

3. Color in the tower and soldier.

4. Place the soldier so that his body is behind the tower and his shield in front.

5. Tape the soldier's body to the back of the tower to hold it in place.

Your bookmark is ready to use!

Later knights

56 **Armored knights were the most important troops.** Knights had the best arms and armor and were the most experienced men in any army, so they were often put in command.

57 **Knights sometimes fought on foot, instead of on horseback.** English knights fought on foot after about 1300. This enabled them to hold a position more securely and co-operate more effectively with other soldiers.

▶ The bascinet helmet had a visor that could be lifted so the wearer could see and breathe.

I DON'T BELIEVE IT!

At the Battle of Agincourt in France in 1415, the English killed 10,000 Frenchmen, but only about 100 Englishmen lost their lives.

58

Horse armor made of metal and leather was introduced to protect horses. By about 1300, knights began to dress their horses in various sorts of armor. Horses without armor could be killed or injured by enemy arrows or spears, leaving the knight open to attack. Men with armored horses were put in the front rank during battle.

▶ Horse armor was shaped to fit the horse's head and neck, then was left loose to dangle down over the legs.

59

The flail was a difficult weapon to use. It consisted of a big metal ball studded with spikes and attached to a chain on a wooden handle. It could inflict terrible injuries, but also swing back unexpectedly, so only men who practised with it for hours each day could use it properly.

◀ A knight uses a flail in foot combat.

60

Each man had his place in battle. Before each battle, the commander would position his men to ensure that the abilities of each were put to best use. The men with the best armor were placed where the enemy was expected to attack, while archers were positioned on the flank (left or right side) where they could shoot across the battlefield. Lightly armored men were held in the rear, ready to chase enemy soldiers if they began to retreat.

Desert warfare

61 Bows were made of many materials. In the desert areas of the Middle East, soldiers used bows made from layers of animal horn, bone, and sinew that were stuck tightly together and then carved into shape. These were called "composite bows," and fired arrows with much greater force than longbows.

▲ The recurved bow was short, but powerful.

62 The Mongols wore light armor. A tribe from central Asia called the Mongols were led by Genghis Khan (1162–1227). Their armor was light because there was a lack of iron in Central Asia. As a result, they developed tactics based on fast-moving cavalry attacks.

63 **Curved swords were known as scimitars.** Armorers working in the city of Damascus, Syria, invented a new way to make swords around the year 1100. This involved folding the steel over on itself several times while the metal was white hot. The new type of steel was used to make curved swords that were both light in weight and incredibly sharp, called scimitars.

64 **Teneke armor was made up of a mail coat onto which were fixed overlapping pieces of flat metal.** These pieces were about 6 inches by 0.5 inches. The plates were loosely hinged so that air could pass through easily but blows from a sword could not. The armor was light, comfortable, and effective, but it was also expensive.

▲ A Saracen wearing teneke armor and wielding a scimitar. The Saracens wore flowing cloaks and turbans to help combat the heat of the desert.

◄ A Mongol army attacks men from the city of Kiev, Ukraine. Although designed for grasslands and deserts, Mongol weaponry was effective in cold forests as well.

65 **Armor was light because of the desert heat.** The plate armor in use in Europe was not worn in the deserts of the Middle East. The plates of metal stopped air circulating around the body and were very uncomfortable to wear. Instead desert fighters in the 13th to 15th centuries wore loose robes and light pieces of armor.

Indian arms

▼ An Indian soldier who wears no armor, but carries a shield and a pata sword.

▶ Indian shields often had intricate designs to make them look more impressive.

66 India had a unique tradition of arms manufacture. Between 1650 and 1800 the vast lands south of the Himalayas, modern India, Pakistan, and Bangladesh, were divided into lots of small states. Each state had its own army, and made great efforts to have impressive weapons.

67 The khanda was a sword with a long, straight blade. These swords had heavy, double-edged blades that often had handles big enough to allow them to be held in both hands. Larger khanda were slung from a belt over the shoulder so that they hung down the user's back.

68 Indian soldiers used the pata. This was an iron glove (gauntlet) that extended almost to the elbow, attached to a sword blade. It was very useful for thrusting, especially when attacking infantry from horseback, but was less effective at cutting.

69 Talwars were curved swords with a single, sharp cutting edge. The handles were often rounded, rather like the butt of a pistol. They were highly decorated with silver, gold, and semi-precious stones.

▲ The talwar sword was invented around AD 1000 and was used in battle for over 900 years.

70 Elephants were used in warfare. A small platform, ("howdah"), was strapped to the back of the elephant. Men armed with bows, or later with guns, sat in the howdah and shot at the enemy over the elephant's head.

▶ War elephants were often covered in armor, while the howdah, in which the soldiers sat, could be covered with iron.

Island wars

71 **Polynesians fought without armor or shields.** The islands in the Pacific Ocean were home to people of the Polynesian culture. Before contact with Europeans around 1750, the Polynesians made their weapons from natural materials. They preferred to rely on skill and movement in battle rather than armor, though some men wore thick shirts of plaited coconut fibers as protection.

72 **Shark teeth were made into swords.** In western Polynesia, shark teeth were added to the sides of long clubs to produce a weapon called the tebutje. This was used to cut as well as smash and was a vicious close-combat weapon.

▼ A Polynesian war canoe on its way to a raid on another island. The warriors paddling the canoe kept their weapons beside them.

▲ Boomerangs often had decorative carvings or were brightly painted.

73 The boomerang didn't always come back.

Native Australian people used spears and bows and arrows, as well as the boomerang. This heavy throwing stick was shaped so that it spun round in the air and could be thrown with accuracy. Only the lighter boomerangs, used for hunting birds, were designed to come back to the thrower.

74 War clubs were favored weapons.

Wooden clubs were carved from single pieces of wood and were over 3 feet in length. They had wide, heavy heads that were often elaborately carved with shapes and patterns.

▶ A Maori mere, or short club. These weapons were made from very hard woods.

75 The Maori used wooden weapons.

The Polynesian people who live in New Zealand are known as the Maori. They produced unique types of club. One type was the mere, which had a short handle and a wide curved blade that could be used for slashing at the enemy.

I DON'T BELIEVE IT!

In the Fiji islands warriors would often use a wooden club shaped like a pineapple to attack their victims.

37

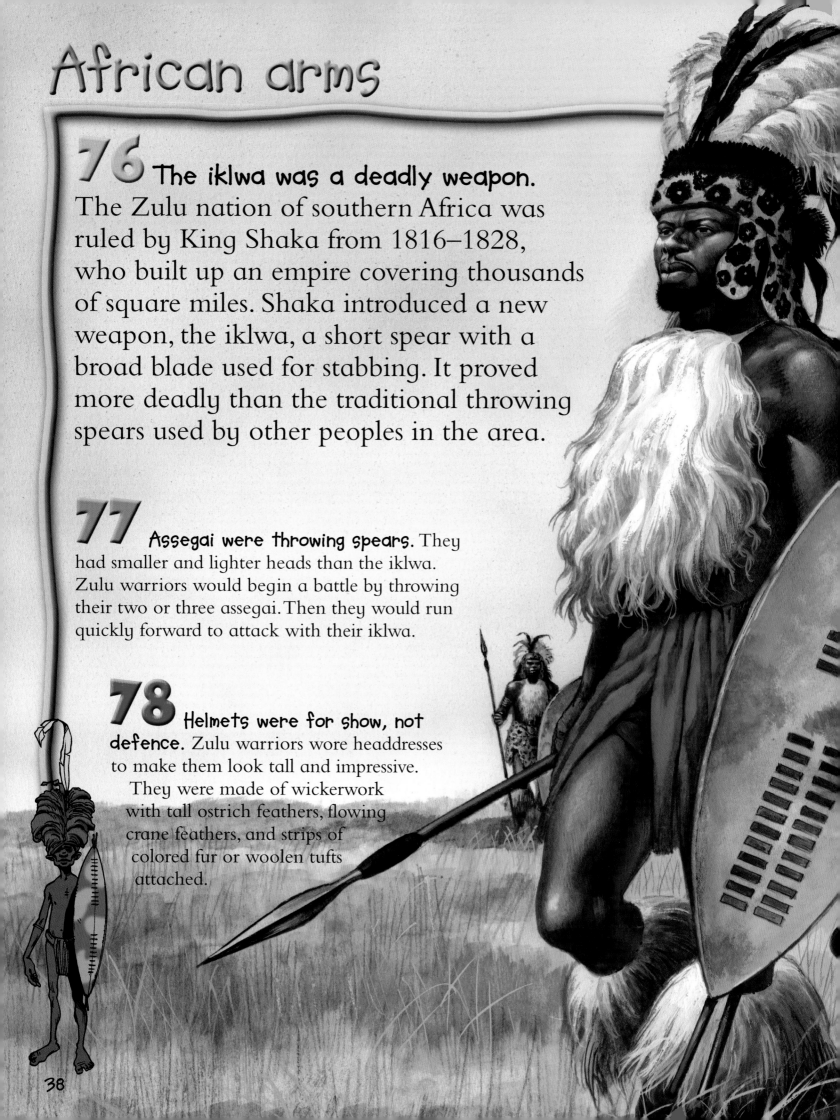

African arms

76 **The iklwa was a deadly weapon.** The Zulu nation of southern Africa was ruled by King Shaka from 1816–1828, who built up an empire covering thousands of square miles. Shaka introduced a new weapon, the iklwa, a short spear with a broad blade used for stabbing. It proved more deadly than the traditional throwing spears used by other peoples in the area.

77 **Assegai were throwing spears.** They had smaller and lighter heads than the iklwa. Zulu warriors would begin a battle by throwing their two or three assegai. Then they would run quickly forward to attack with their iklwa.

78 **Helmets were for show, not defence.** Zulu warriors wore headdresses to make them look tall and impressive. They were made of wickerwork with tall ostrich feathers, flowing crane feathers, and strips of colored fur or woolen tufts attached.

79

Knobkerries could crush skulls. Many Zulu warriors carried a heavy wooden club, or knobkerrie, as well as the iklwa. If the iklwa was lost, the knobkerrie could be used for close fighting.

80

Shields were made of cowhide. Zulu shields were nearly 6 feet in length, and were cut from cowhide, which was laced onto a central wooden pole with strips of leather.

Make Zulu puppets

You will need:
card • ice-lolly sticks
crayons • glue

1. Draw some Zulu warriors onto card.
2. Cut out each of the warriors and color them in.
3. Glue an ice-lolly stick to the back of each warrior.
4. If you make enough Zulus, glue the lolly sticks to a straight piece of wood so that the warriors form a rank.

◄ A Zulu impi, or army, on the march. Boys followed the warriors carrying bedding, food, and spare weapons.

39

The Americas

81 In South America, spears were thrown at the start of a battle. The Aztec people built up a large empire in what is now Mexico between 1400 and 1510. Their warriors won a series of battles against other American peoples. Each battle began with men on both sides throwing light javelins at the enemy. Then the men would charge at each other to fight at close quarters.

◄ In battle, some Aztec warriors dressed as eagles, jaguars, and other fierce animals.

82 Obsidian stone was razor sharp. The Aztec, Maya, and other peoples of South America did not know how to make iron or bronze, so they made their weapons from natural materials. The most effective weapons were edged with slivers of obsidian, a hard, glasslike stone that has a very sharp edge when first broken.

83 **Clubs were used to knock enemies unconscious.** One of the main purposes of warfare among the Maya and Aztec people was to capture prisoners. The prisoners were then taken to temples to be sacrificed to gods such as Huitzilopochtli, the god of war, by having their hearts cut out while still beating.

84 **Shields were highly decorated.** The shields used by Aztec and Maya warriors were made of wood, and covered with brightly colored animal skins and feathers. They often had strings of feathers or fur dangling down underneath to deflect javelins.

◄ The Maya tried to capture enemy noblemen and rulers to use as sacrifices to the gods.

85 **The tomahawk was a famous weapon of the North American tribes.** This was a short-handled ax with a heavy head. The first tomahawks were made with stone heads, but after Europeans reached North America, the tribes began buying steel-headed tomahawks.

► The native peoples of the eastern areas of North America used spears and special axes, known as tomahawks.

The code of Bushido

86 **Samurai wore elaborate armor.** From around 800–1860, warriors known as the samurai ruled the islands of Japan. Samurai wore suits of armor made from hundreds of small plates of metal laced together with silk. Each group of samurai had a badge, or sashimono, which was often a picture of a plant or animal.

87 **The swords of the samurai took weeks to make.** The samurai sword was produced by blending strips of different types of steel, and shaping them to produce a smooth blade. Each sword was made by a master craftsman in a process that involved prayers and religious rituals as well as metalwork.

88 **Bushido was the way of the warrior.** By around 1500 the samurai were expected to follow a code of behavior known as Bushido, which demanded loyalty and honor as well as bravery and skill with weapons.

▲ The samurai practised with weapons and armor for long periods. They sometimes exercised with elaborate displays.

Make Sashimono flags

You will need:
rectangles of A4 colored paper
scissors • string • crayons

1. Fold each piece of paper in half.
2. On both sides of each piece of paper draw an animal or plant.
3. Hang each piece of paper over the string at the fold to make a line of flags.
4. Hang the flags up in your room.

▲ All samurai were trained in mounted combat and were expected to use their bows as well as their swords when riding at a gallop.

89 **Archery was a great skill.**
Around AD 800, the earliest samurai called their profession 'the path of the arrow'. This was because skill at archery was thought to be the most important for a warrior. Swords later became more important, but archery remained a key skill until the end of the samurai period in the 1860s.

90 **Most samurai carried two swords.** The katana was most often used in combat, while the shorter wakizashi was used in an emergency or for ritual suicide. Some samurai preferred the much longer two-handed nodachi sword when going into battle.

► A print of a samurai warrior showing the brightly patterned clothes that the warriors liked to wear.

The end of an era

A wheel-lock pistol from about 1650. The wheel-lock was the first reliable firing mechanism.

91 **The first guns could not penetrate heavy armor.** Early forms of gunpowder were not powerful enough to shoot a bullet from a hand-held gun with much force. By 1600, armorers were producing helmets and breastplates that were bulletproof.

92 **Cannons could destroy armor.** Large cannons fired iron or stone balls that weighed up to 55 pounds. They were designed to knock down stone walls, but were also used in battle. No armor could survive being hit by such a weapon.

◄ A musketeer in about 1660. Each cartridge on his belt holds a bullet and powder to fire it.

93 **Cavalry continued to wear body armor.** Until 1914, cavalry engaged in fast-moving fights could often not reload their guns once they had been fired. As a result cavalrymen often fought using swords and lances, so armor was still useful.

▼ A French cavalryman in 1810. He wears an iron helmet and iron body armor.

94 **Infantry officers wore gorget armor.** This was one of the last kinds of armor to be worn. It was a small piece of armor that fitted under the front of the helmet and protected the neck. Gorgets were often used to show the rank of the man wearing them, so they continued to be worn long after helmets were abandoned. They were used until 1914 in some countries.

▶ A musketeer in about 1770. He is using a ramrod to push the bullet and gunpowder down the barrel of a gun before firing it.

95 **By 1850 most soldiers no longer wore armor.** As guns became more effective, they were able to fire bullets with greater accuracy over longer distances and with more power. By 1850 most infantry were armed with guns that could shoot through any type of armor, so most soldiers stopped wearing armor.

I DON'T BELIEVE IT!

As late as 1914 some French cavalry went to war wearing armor, despite the fact that they had to face artillery and machine guns.

Modern arms and armor

96 The first modern use of chemical weapons was in World War I. In April 1915, the Germans used poison gas against French soldiers. It worked by irritating the lining of the lungs and throat. Soldiers then began to wear anti-gas uniforms as protection.

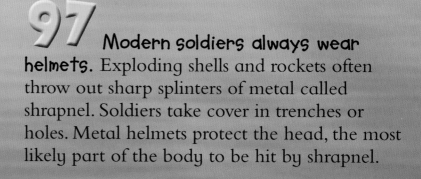

▶ A British infantryman in 1944. He wears a steel helmet and carries a Sten gun—a light machine gun.

▲ A British cavalryman charges in 1916. Both the man and horse wear gas masks to protect them against poison gas.

QUIZ

1. Was poisoned gas first used in World War II?
2. What does APC stand for?
3. Do bomb disposal men wear special anti-blast armor?

Answers:
1. No. It was first used in World War I 2. Armoured Personnel Carrier 3. Yes

97 Modern soldiers always wear helmets. Exploding shells and rockets often throw out sharp splinters of metal called shrapnel. Soldiers take cover in trenches or holes. Metal helmets protect the head, the most likely part of the body to be hit by shrapnel.

► A Main Battle Tank (MBT) advances through the desert. The arrival of tanks and other armored vehicles has transformed modern warfare.

98 **Modern armored warfare involves tanks.** The armor needed to stop modern shells and rockets is too heavy for a person to carry, but it can be mounted on a vehicle, such as a tank or an armored personnel carrier (APC). These vehicles are the key feature of a modern army, as the armored knights were in the middle ages.

99 **The best armor makes you disappear.** Camouflage conceals soldiers by using colors that blend into the background of plants, sky, or sand. Helmets often have a strap that can be used to attach vegetation for extra camouflage.

▼ An American soldier in Iraq. He wears bulletproof body armor as well as a helmet.

100 **Bomb disposal soldiers use special armor.** Designed to give protection against blast waves, the armor covers as much of the body as possible while still allowing the soldier to use his hands to defuse the bomb.

Index